How Product Managers Can Grow Their Career

How Product Managers Can Find And
Succeed In The Right Job

*"Practical, proven examples of how to secure the
right product management job and be a success!"*

Dr. Jim Anderson

Published by:
Blue Elephant Consulting
Tampa, Florida

Printed in the United States of America

Library of Congress Control Number: 2014950748

ISBN-13: 978-1502301901
ISBN-10: 1502301903

Warning – Disclaimer

Recent Books By
The Author

Product Management

- Product Management Secrets: Techniques For Product Managers To Boost Product Sales And Increase Customer Satisfaction

- Customer Lessons For Product Managers: Techniques For Product Managers To Better Understand What Their Customers Really Want

Public Speaking

- How To Become A Better Speaker By Changing How You Speak: Change techniques that will transform a speech into a memorable event

- How To Give A Great Presentation: Presentation techniques that will transform a speech into a memorable event

CIO Skills

- What CIOs Need To Know About Working With Partners: Techniques For CIOs To Use In Order To Be Able To Successfully Work With Partners

- How CIOs Can Make Innovation Happen: Tips And Techniques For CIOs To Use In Order To Make Innovation Happen In Their IT Department

IT Manager Skills

- How IT Managers Can Make Innovation Happen: Tips And Techniques For IT Managers To Use In Order To Make Innovation Happen In Their Teams

- Secrets Of Effective Leadership For IT Managers: Tips And Techniques That IT Managers Can Use In Order To Develop Leadership Skills

Negotiating

- Learn How To Signal In Your Next Negotiation: How To Develop The Skill Of Effective Signaling In A Negotiation In Order To Get The Best Possible Outcome

- Learn The Skill Of Exploring In A Negotiation: How To Develop The Skill Of Exploring What Is Possible In A Negotiation In Order To Reach The Best Possible Deal

Miscellaneous

- The Internet-Enabled Successful School District Superintendent: How To Use The Internet To Boost Parental Involvement In Your Schools

- Power Distribution Unit (PDU) Secrets: What Everyone Who Works In A Data Center Needs To Know!

Note: See a complete list of books by Dr. Jim Anderson at the back of this book.

Acknowledgements

Any book like this one is the result of years of real-world work experience. In my over 25 years of working for 7 different firms, I have met countless fantastic people and I've been mentored by some truly exceptional ones. Although I've probably forgotten some of the people who made me the person that I am today, here is my attempt to finally give them the recognition that they so truly deserve:

- Thomas P. Anderson
- Art Puett
- Bobbi Marshall
- Bob Boggs

Dr. Jim Anderson

This book is dedicated to my wife Lori. None of this would have been possible without her love and support.

Thanks for the best 21 years of my life (so far)...!

Speaking.   Negotiating.   Managing.   Marketing.

Table Of Contents

It's All About The Product

I happen to think that being a product manager is one of the best jobs out there. I find it to be very satisfying because I'm in charge of the success of a product.

If I do the right things, then my product will be selected by a large number of customers and it will solve their problems. If I don't do my job right, my company will probably decide to stop offering my product after a while. Ultimately, my career is in my hands.

As product managers, we all control our careers. What this means is that we need to always be networking because you never know when you may find yourself looking for your next job. As we move through our career, it will soon be important that we learn how to not only manage products, but people also.

The way that we land a product manager job is by having a resume that does the work for us. How to create such a resume is a skill that we all have to learn. We don't know it all and so in order to help us to make the right decisions, it can be helpful to find a mentor who is willing to give us good advice.

Once we've landed the right job, our work is not over. We need to understand how to get things done effectively and multitasking is not the answer. Additionally, if despite our hard work we get passed over for the next promotion we need to have a plan as to what our next steps are going to be.

For more information on what it takes to be a great product manager, check out my blog, The Accidental Product Manager, at:

www.TheAccidentalPM.com

Good luck!

-    Dr. Jim Anderson

About The Author

I must confess that I never set out to be a product manager. When I went to school, I studied Computer Science and thought that I'd get a nice job programming and that would be that. Well, at least part of that plan worked out!

My first job was working for Boeing on their F/A-18 fighter jet program. I spent my days programming fighter jet software in assembly language and I loved it. The U.S. government decided to save some money and went looking for other countries to sell this plane to. This put me into an unfamiliar role: I started to meet with foreign military officials in order to explain what my product did.

Time moved on and so did I. I found myself working for Siemens, the big German telecommunications company. They were making phone switches and selling them to the seven U.S. phone companies. The problem was that the switches were too complicated. Customers couldn't tell the difference between one complicated phone switch from another complicated phone switch.

The Siemens sales folks were in a bind. They didn't know enough about how the switches worked to tell their customers why they should buy them. Siemens reached out into their engineering unit looking for anyone who could help the sales teams out. I put my hand up and overnight I became a product manager.

Since then I've spent over 20 years working as a product manager for both big companies and startups. This has given me an opportunity to do everything that a product manager does many, many times. I know what works as well as what doesn't work.

I now live in Tampa Florida where I spend my time managing my consulting business, Blue Elephant Consulting, teaching college courses at the University of South Florida, and traveling to work with companies like yours to share the knowledge that I have about how product managers can make their product be a success.

I'm always available to answer questions and I can be reached at:

Dr. Jim Anderson
Blue Elephant Consulting
Email: jim@BlueElephantConsulting.com
Facebook: http://goo.gl/1TVoK
Web: **www.BlueElephantConsulting.com**

**"Unforgettable communication skills that will
set your ideas free..."**

Create Products Your Customers Want At A Price That They Are Willing To Pay!

Dr. Jim Anderson is available to provide training and coaching on the two topics that are the most important to product managers everywhere: how do I create the products that my customers want and what should I price them at?

Dr. Anderson believes that in order to both learn and remember what he says, product managers need to laugh. Each one of his speeches is full of fun and humor so that what he says "sticks" with everyone.

Dr. Anderson's Product Management Training Includes:

1. How can you segment your market?
2. What problems are your customers having right now?
3. Which of your customer's problems does your product solve?
4. How much of this problem does your product solve?
5. How much will it cost your customer if they don't fix this problem?

Dr. Jim Anderson presents over 100 speeches per year. To invite Dr. Anderson to speak at your event, contact him at:

Phone: 813-418-6970 or
Email: jim@BlueElephantConsulting.com

Blue Elephant Consulting
Speaking. Negotiating. Managing. Marketing.

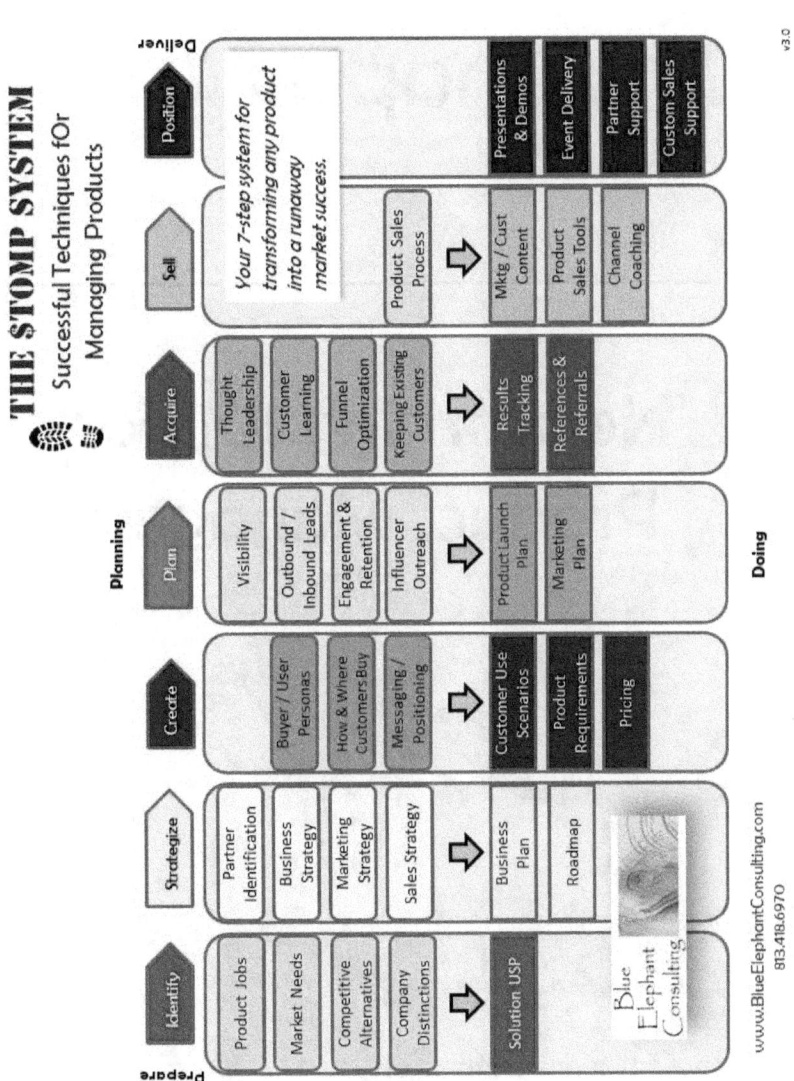

THE $TOMP SYSTEM
Successful Techniques fOr Managing Products

Your 7-step system for transforming any product into a runaway market success.

Prepare | **Planning** | **Doing** | **Deliver**

Identify	Strategize	Create	Plan	Acquire	Sell	Position
Product Jobs	Partner Identification	Buyer / User Personas	Visibility	Thought Leadership	Product Sales Process	Presentations & Demos
Market Needs	Business Strategy	How & Where Customers Buy	Outbound / Inbound Leads	Customer Learning	Mktg / Cust Content	Event Delivery
Competitive Alternatives	Marketing Strategy	Messaging / Positioning	Engagement & Retention	Funnel Optimization	Product Sales Tools	Partner Support
Company Distinctions	Sales Strategy		Influencer Outreach	Keeping Existing Customers	Channel Coaching	Custom Sales Support
Solution USP	Business Plan	Customer Use Scenarios	Product Launch Plan	Results Tracking		
	Roadmap	Product Requirements	Marketing Plan	References & Referrals		
		Pricing				

www.BlueElephantConsulting.com
813.418.6970

Blue Elephant Consulting

v3.0

The **$TOMP** product management system has been created by **Blue Elephant Consulting** to help product managers know what to do and when to do it in order for a product to be successful.

Chapter 1

Networking 101 For Product Managers

Chapter 1: Networking 101 For Product Managers

I don't care if you're the best Product Manager this world has ever known, you may still find yourself without a job sometime – especially in this economy. Yeah, yeah we all know that we should have been **networking like crazy** all along. However, the sad truth is that all too often we neglect this career responsibility until it's too late and we're out on the street. What's a Product Manager to do then?

I'm sure that even the worst networkers among you have a stack of other people's business cards somewhere. The sad truth is that every day our networks get **just a bit more out of date**. If you were to go through your current list of contacts, how many of those do you think would have moved on to new jobs and phone numbers / email addresses?

The reality of a modern Product Manager's life is that you always have to be ready to move on. You may not see the end of your current job coming; however, when it comes you need to make sure that it is no surprise to you. The new career rule is that you always have to **be ready to move at a moment's notice**.

So how do you jump start a professional network that you've allowed to grow old? The first step is to **find the people who WERE in your network**. There are many different ways to do this:

- Email them (often there may be an auto reply with their new email address)

- Use the Internet to search for them – this is when it's great to have contacts with unusually spelled names!

- Ask coworkers to reconnect you to people that they've stayed in touch with better than you.

Need I mention online professional social networks like LinkedIn and Plaxo? These days everyone seems to be using these and one of the nice benefits is that once you connect to someone, you'll be able to reach them **even if they change jobs**.

Chapter 2

Pay Attention Product Manager!

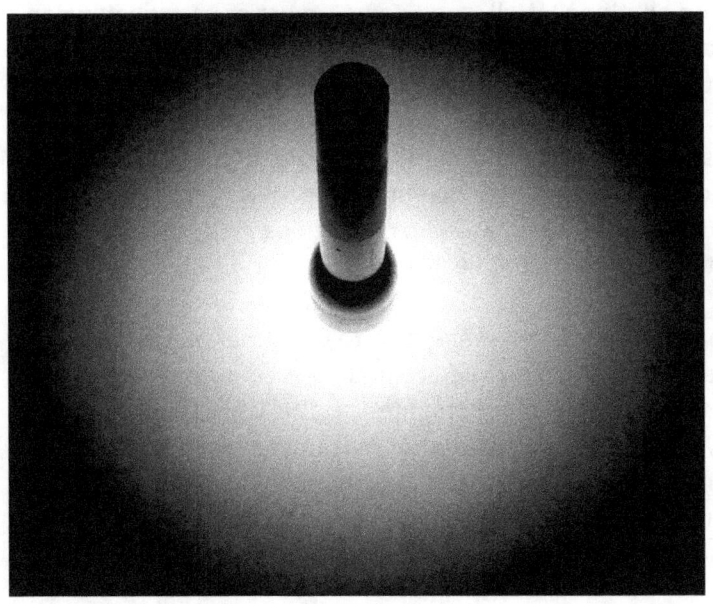

Chapter 2: Pay Attention Product Manager!

So what things are demanding your attention even as you read these words: emails, Web sites, your BlackBerry, text messages, Tweets, cell phone calls, ... so much for having the ability to **pay enough attention** to get any work done.

Wouldn't it be nice if we knew how to keep our minds on something long enough **to make progress** on our products? Well good news, Winifred Gallagher has written a book called Rapt: Attention and the Focused Life in which she investigates our mind's capacity to pay attention.

Look, don't we all feel like those attention deficit disorder (ADD) little kids – we keep getting distracted and just can't seem to focus on anything? Well, good news – most of us probably don't have a medical problem. Instead, we've probably been trying to **multitask** just a bit too much.

Here's the key thing: your mental attention is like **a flashlight in a dark room** – we can only point it towards a thin slice of what surrounds us at any time. When something new catches our attention, we point that flashlight in a different direction.

So what can product managers do to boost our ability for focused attention? You need to find ways to push yourself close to the very edge of your competence. This will then require you to pay close attention. Note that researchers have discovered that the difference between being overwhelmed (stressed out) and underwhelmed (bored) is a fine line. When you're there, they say that you are **in the "zone"**.

If you want to be a better product manager, Gallagher says that you should:

- Start to practice **meditation** - it calms you and allows you to focus on the future.

- **Pause** and be aware of the here and now.

- Cultivate your **willpower** - just like a muscle, it will get stronger the more you use it.

- Eliminate those **distractions** that you can control.

Chapter 3

Your Mother Was Right: How Product Managers Dress For Success

Chapter 3: Your Mother Was Right: How Product Managers Dress For Success

So if you could wear anything that you wanted to work, what would it be? Would you be showing up in shorts and flip-flops? How about jeans and a T-shirt? Well why don't you? The answer to this question is something that we normally don't spend a lot of time thinking about, but because it can have **a big impact on our careers**, perhaps we should...

What, Me Worry?

The first issue that we need to tackle is trying to figure out why there is an issue in the first place. Face it, although we've always been told not to judge someone **by the clothes that they wear**, we all do it anyway.

That's why how you go about dressing can determine how the people that you interact with perceive you while you are at work. Additionally, it can have a big impact in how you feel about yourself. I almost hate to say it, but it's true, how you dress can have an effect on your ability to **get a job** in the first place.

That Professional Look – For Women

I've done some asking around and when I opened my mouth, I got dumped on. There are too few women working as Product Managers and this is clearly an **emotionally charged** topic for many of them. I listened to everyone (for quite some time if I do say so myself), and here are the top four suggestions that were brought up over and over again:

Hose Rule: It turns out that pantyhose (remember them?) are still important. In today's workplace, bare legs send the wrong message – they aren't considered to be professional. Even if they are not required, they are required.

Shoe Time: This one sorta lost me because I just don't pay enough attention to shoes. However, smarter people than I told me that regular sandals and even open-toed shoes are *generally* considered to be acceptable for the workplace. However, the ultra-comfortable flip-flops and toe-post sandals (what are those?) are not.

Tall Patterns: Those women who are tall have a bit of a challenge especially if they work with / for shorter men – their height can make them appear overpowering. The goal here is to not emphasize what you already have – height. Instead, go with a horizontal pattern.

Short Patterns: The goal here is to attempt to buy yourself some height so that you don't have to kill yourself wearing 4" heels all the time. The suggestion is that wearing a cropped jacket can help make your legs appear longer.

That Professional Look – For Men

Ok, so we've pointed out what women need to do to make the clothes that they wear to the office work for them, **not against them**. Now let's see if we can do the same for men:

Watch The Boss: One of the most important things that you can do is to watch what the boss wears and match him. This is especially important on so-called "casual days".

Super Dressy (Sorta): Things have changed. The #1 dressy look in the office these days is wearing a suit, but with no tie.

Sports: You can't go wrong if you wear a sport coat. The experts recommend that you go with either earth or gray tones in order to make matching with shirts easier.

Pants: There always seems to be too many choices here. Stick with medium to dark worsted wool and you can't go wrong.

Final Thoughts

Mom was right after all – clothes do make the man / woman. Dressing well **sends a message** to others that says "if I care enough to take the time to dress this way, just imagine how much time I'll take to solve your problems." Now that's the right message to be sending!

Chapter 4

Grow Your Career – What Product Managers Need To Do For Success

Chapter 4: Grow Your Career – What Product Managers Need To Do For Success

As though the job of being a Product Manager was not hard enough, there's also that added responsibility that you have to manage your career. With all of the turmoil of the past couple of years, it's now more important than ever for Product Managers to find the time to tend to this task.

Growing Your Career – It's Like Another Job

The #1 thing that Product Managers need to realize is that it is no longer good enough to sit passively by and hope that your career will take you to someplace that you want to be. Instead, you need to take charge of it. Yes, this means that there is more work for you to do. However, you will benefit from all of the time and effort that you put into this task.

It's Networking Time

For some odd reason too many of us shun what is probably the most effective career management activity – networking. Study after study has shown that most high paying professional jobs are found through networking. What this means for you is that you need to always be growing your network.

This might cause you to rush out and try to build the largest LinkedIn network that you possibly can. Don't do it. Deborah Bailey, who is a career and employment coach, points out that the quality of the members of your professional network is far more important than quantity of people that you have in the network.

Get Uncomfortable

We all chose to have a career in product management for a bunch of reasons. One of these was because we knew that it was a dynamic field – it's always changing. What this means for you is that you can't sit back and assume that the skills that you have today (both hard and soft skills) will be what anyone will be looking for tomorrow.

Instead, you need to get up off your butt and go out and learn something new. This ability to be constantly seeking out new things to learn will be what keeps your skills fresh and makes sure that you are always employable.

Big Picture Stuff

This might be the trickiest part of the program – learning to keep your eyes open. It's all too easy to focus on what's going on inside of your company or even within your industry. However, the key to long-term career success is to stay on top of what's going on in the big world and understand how it may impact your company and your career.

Final Thoughts

You have no control over what others may do to your career in the future. However, you have complete control over what you do to prepare your career for the future. You are going to need to be proactive (start doing something TODAY) and you are going to have to be willing to adapt to the changes that we all know will happen in the product management field. If you can do both of these things, you will have truly taken control of your career.

Chapter 5

How Can Product Managers Manage People?

Chapter 5: How Can Product Managers Manage People?

So what do product managers manage? Generally I'd agree with you if you answered "**products**"; however, I've been giving this some thought and I think that we're missing the mark if that's our answer.

If you think about it, what we really spend our time doing is **managing people** and hoping that they will help us to make our products successful. That being said, did you ever get any training on how to manage people?

Product Managers Don't Make Beautiful Music

One of the more popular ways to think about the how product managers do their job is to picture them as being orchestra conductors. You can almost imagine yourself standing in front of everyone who works for your company, tapping your conductor's wand on the sheet music stand in front of you, and then with a flourish you begin.

First up is the requirements team, before they are done the product developers step in followed by marketing and sales softly at first and then louder as time moves on. Nice **mental picture**, eh?

Too bad life doesn't really work out this way. Dr. Henry Mintzberg at McGill University says that in reality what you'd be hearing is what a pre-concert warm-up sounds like – everyone **out of tune** and playing over the top of each other. Now that's what I am familiar with!

Dr. Mintzberg points out that each and every one of us is **flawed** - there is no such thing as a perfect product manager. However, the really good product managers are less screwed-up and that is something that we can shoot for.

It's All About the Interruptions

Think about how your yesterday went. Did you start the day with a plan and then were you able to accomplish that plan? I'm willing to bet that the answer is probably not.   It's a fact of life for the modern product manager that every day is basically **a stream of interruptions** – one after another.

Don't even get me started on what Blackberries and email have done to compound the interruption problem. One top of this madness we need to find a way to manage the people that we work with – and it sure looks like we're doing it **the wrong way**.

The Three Planes of Product Management

Product managers are **never taught** how to manage people to get results. This means that too many of us end up hiding behind emails and sticky notes when we are trying to get our virtual teams to accomplish tasks.

Dr. Mintzberg has identified three different "**planes**" of how we can manage people. We need to use all three, but we are currently not balancing how we use them.

The Direct Plane – this is where product managers "get their hands dirty" and jump right in and manage actions directly. You know what this looks like – we manage projects, we negotiate contracts. In all honesty this is the easiest way to do things because we don't have to go through the effort of getting others to do work for us.

The Manage People Plane – this is the tricky one. If product managers can find the time, then they can work with the people that they need to take action in order to make their product a success and motivate them, train them, build teams, etc. In other words, make it so that they can take action and be more effective. Easy to say, hard to do.

The Manage Information Plane – all too often this is where product managers choose to hide out. Here we can manage information in order to drive people. We use budgets and objectives, we delegate tasks, set organizational structures, etc. All very powerful stuff, but note that we don't necessarily have to deal with real people and all of the messy issues that that might entail.

Final Thoughts

Nobody ever taught you how to manage the people that you need to convince to do **what you need them to do** in order to make your product a success. You've probably discovered by now that you've got a lot of different ways to make things happen.

The worst kind of product manager manages **only by using information**. Sure this is a comfortable way of doing things and seems to be the simplest way to get things accomplished. However, it's always better to spend the time **working with the people** that you need on your side. In the end you'll be glad that you did.

Product managers who can do this will have found yet another way that great product managers make their product(s) **fantastically successful**.

Chapter 6

You Don't Do a Good Job at Multitasking Product Manager, Get Over It

Chapter 6: You Don't Do A Good Job At Multitasking Product Manager, Get Over It

Too little time, too much to do. Does that adequately describe your product manager job? I don't know about you, but often is the time that I've looked with envy at my peers who are great **multitaskers** and wished that I could be more like them. It turns out that I was wishing for the wrong thing – multitaskers actually do a **lousy job** at just about everything.

The Study

Ruth Pennenaker reports that some researchers at Stanford University have just completed a groundbreaking study on **people who multitask**. You know who you are – you're talking on the phone even as you are answering emails and zipping off text messages on your iPhone all at the same time. Oh how I have so wanted to be you!

The researchers found that most persistent multitaskers actually **performed badly** in a variety of tasks that they were asked to do. As the researchers dove deeper to find out why the multitaskers were doing so badly, what they found was that they don't do a very good job of focusing on what they are trying to do. This also means that they are much more likely to get distracted while they are trying to perform a task. On top of all this, the study showed that they are actually weaker than non-multitaskers at shifting between tasks and organizing the information that they collect.

Results Of The Study

My favorite part of the study is where the researchers discovered that people who are always multitasking are actually

worse at multitasking than those of us who ordinarily don't multitask!

When the study was started, the researchers started with the idea that multitaskers have some characteristic that makes them **better at multitasking** than regular folks. What they discovered is that multitaskers are just pretty much lousy at doing everything.

One of the researchers was quoted as saying "We kept looking for multitaskers' advantages in this study. But we kept finding only disadvantages. We thought multitaskers were very much in control of information. It turns out, they were just **getting it all confused**."

However, doesn't it LOOK like multitaskers are always busy? Shouldn't that mean that they must be getting more done than the rest of us who just can't do that much all at the same time? It turns out that high multitaskers are "**suckers for irrelevancy**". Simply put, sure they are doing things, but what they are working on more often than not really doesn't matter.

A Personal Multitasking (Failure) Story

I firmly fall into the "not a good multasker" camp and I should know it. However, every once in a while I try my hand at multitasking, generally with **disastrous results**. Allow me to share my most recent story:

I was **late for a doctor's appointment** and yet I had a conference call that I needed to participate in (not just listen to). I jumped into the car, programmed the Garmin GPS system with the doctor's office address, stuck my Blackberry headset in my ear, and set the Garmin on "mute" so that it wouldn't interfere with my conference call.

As I hurtled down the highway in the far left lane at about 70 mph jabbering away in an animated conversation on the conference call, I happened to look over at the Garmin and noticed that it was signaling that I needed to be **taking the exit** that I was just about to pass by (remember that I had been smart enough to mute it so I had no warning). Oh, oh.

A non-multitasking person would have realized that: (1) I had already gone too far past the exit to make it, (2) I was in the wrong lane to try to make the exit, (3) I was going too fast to make the exit. In my multitasking state, I **realized none of this** and I attempted to go for it.

I didn't make it. I was going too fast and I was too far past the exit to have ever had any chance of making it. What I ended up doing was **plowing headfirst** into the aluminum guardrails which were anchored to solid 4"x4" chunks of wood. I probably hit them going a good 40 mph despite having tried to stand on the brakes once I realized what was going to happen.

Thanks to seatbelts and airbags, I walked away without a scratch. However, the car was a **total loss**. Oh, and I got a $100+ ticket from the police for basically being a bad driver. I say once again – I can't multitask!

Final Thoughts

Product managers who multitask will perform at a lower level than product managers who focus on one task at a time. Although this seems to fly in the face of everything that we've seen in our workplace (don't multitaskers get all of the promotions?), you can't argue with research results.

Should you try to convince your friends and peers who are multitaskers to stop doing it because it just doesn't work? No. The core of the problem is that not only do multitaskers **think**

they're great at what they do; they've also convinced everybody else they're good at it too.

Ultimately those of us who are not multitaskers will be able to show better results for how we've spent our time. If we can make sure that the rules of the game that we're playing are **all about results** and not appearances, then the non-multitaskers will win every time.

Product managers who can focus on one task at a time and do it well instead of trying to do multiple tasks at the same time poorly will have found yet another way that great product managers make their product(s) **fantastically successful**.

Chapter 7

How To Build A Mentor Network For Your Product Management Career

Chapter 7: How To Build A Mentor Network For Your Product Management Career

I've got a quick question for you: what is the next step in your career? What do you want to get promoted to? In fact, as long as we are talking about that, what comes after THAT promotion? In product management the career ladder generally goes: product manager, director, executive director, VP of marketing, Sr. VP, CEO. Got a plan on how you are going to get to that next step?

The Problem With Product Manager Career Mentors

It used to be that what you needed in order to climb out of a product management position was a mentor - someone who would take you under their wing and guide you during your career. Bad news – those days are long gone.

It wasn't that there was anything wrong with the old way, it's just that the world started to move faster. Nowadays nobody stays in a given position long enough to act as a mentor to you for any reasonable length of time. Even if they did, they are probably too busy to spend enough time with you in order to keep your career on track.

The old way of picking a mentor and having them work with you over time to shape and guide your career is gone – things move too fast and change too often to allow this to work anymore. Instead, product managers need to discover how to create networks of mentors that they can use to provide the career guidance that they will need over the years.

If you thought the old way was tough, just wait until you try to figure out how to do things using the new way!

The New Way Of Managing Your Career

Dr. Dawn Chandler (CA Polytech State University), Dr. Douglas Hall (Boston University) and Dr. Kathy Kram (Boston University) have spent some time looking into this problem with the modern product management workplace and they've got some ideas about how we can fix things.

Since there is really no way for you to get a single individual to agree to act as your mentor for the 40-45 years that your product management career is going to last, instead you are going to have to take a different approach. You are going to have to create a network of mentors that you can use to accomplish what you need to get done.

Oh, there is one small problem with this clever solution: most of us are not all that good at creating a mentor network like this let alone trying to maintain it. It looks like you are going to need some suggestions on how best to do this.

Building And Maintaining A Mentor Network

One of the first things that you are going to have to realize about building your mentor network is that the people that you are going to ask to be a part of your network will not all be the same. This means that you are going to have to develop a special set of skills in order to be able to (1) find them, and (2) create relationships with them that will make them want to mentor you.

Here is what you are going to have to do in order to create a mentoring network that will help your product management career move to the next level:

Talk, Talk,Talk - you are going to have to be willing to take the initiative and reach out to those people that you want to be a part of your mentoring network – they aren't going to contact you. Once you've contacted them the first time, then you are going to have to work at maintaining contact with them so that they don't forget about you.

Be Sensitive – Not everyone that you talk to is going to want to be your mentor. It's going to be up to you to take the time to pick up on the message that they are sending your way. Few people will actually come out and say "no", so it's up to you to detect those folks who would like to decline the opportunity.

It's The Takeoff That Counts – when you've found someone who is willing to be a member of your mentor network, you've got to be willing to make an extra effort to make sure that your initial interactions with that person go very well. They will set tone for the rest of your relationship. Show up early for meetings, follow up quickly on actions, and pay attention when they are talking.

Be Prepared – make sure that you get ready for every meeting with someone who is in your mentor network. Research what you want to ask them, make sure that you can show that you are making progress in your career, and come prepared to ask questions about challenges that you are currently facing.

Information Is The Key – you need to be willing to share information with your mentoring network. This does not mean that you have to tell them all the details about what you had for breakfast today, but rather that you be willing to lay out your current challenges and failures that you've had – you know, stuff that can be hard to talk about.

It's A Two-Way Street – if someone agrees to be a part of your mentoring network, then you have agreed to do your best to help them out also. This means that you have a responsibility to help your mentors out whenever you have an opportunity to do so. This can be as simple as passing on information that you run across to actually doing work for them.

Be A Nice Person – Nobody want to work with a jerk and they certainly don't want to mentor one. No matter what kind of day you've had, always be on your best behavior when you interact with a member of your mentor network.

Be Positive – how you choose to view the world is a key part of how others see you. If you have a positive attitude you will naturally attract people to your mentor network and you'll be able to keep them there. If you've got a negative attitude, then nobody is going to want to lend you a helping hand.

Final Thoughts

As a product manager you are undoubtedly busy. However, it turns out that you have yet another job on top of your "day job" – managing your career. You can't do this by yourself and so you're going to need to have someone guide you – a mentor network.

Creating and maintaining a mentor network is no easy task. However, if you go about doing it in the right way it can become a powerful force that will cause your career to shoot ahead and make sure that you don't get left behind.

Product managers who can do this will have found yet another way that great product managers make their product(s) fantastically successful.

Chapter 8

Let's Go Job Shopping: What A Product Manager Needs To Have On Their Resume

Chapter 8: Let's Go Job Shopping: What A Product Manager Needs To Have On Their Resume

As the global recession starts to fade away, product managers who are searching for a new job are starting to feel some new hope and product managers who still have jobs are starting to get the itch to take a look around at what other opportunities there might be out there. Sounds like it's time to get some resumes in order...

Overall Format

A quick search of the Internet will reveal suggestions for a large number of different formats for resumes: classic, modern, etc. What is the right format for you? Sure, if you are applying to a progressive firm, a novel formatted resume might be eye catching, but since you can never tell what they are really looking for I'm going to suggest that you stick with the classic format.

This means that you should start out with your contact information and follow it up with a summary statement. After this you should list out your career in reverse chronological order (what you've done most recently is always the most interesting). Each job needs to be described by a list of bullet points. Wrap things up by listing your educational accomplishments.

Things That Need To Be In Your Resume

Ok, so clearly your resume needs to be both well-organized and easy to read. The person who will be reading it will probably be moving quickly and if your resume is hard to read, they won't read it. Depending on how long you've been working, a three-page resume is just fine – you've probably done a lot and so there's a lot for you to document.

We live in a world where more often than not resumes now get scanned by computers before a human ever lays eyes on them. What this means is you've got to write your resume in such a way that a computer can process it correctly. This means that you've got to load it with keywords that recruiters would be using when searching for candidates. You can figure out what these keywords are by taking a look at job descriptions for the types of jobs that you are looking for – work the words used to describe the job into your resume.

In the world of product management we use a lot of acronyms to describe technologies and certifications. Feel free to include the acronyms in your resume, but make sure that you also spell them out at least once.

Three Things To Avoid

It's all too easy to get caught up in worrying about what font to use and how to cram everything that you've done into as small of a space as possible. However, spending too much time on things that don't matter can easily let a product manager skip over three things that are important. Here they are:

- **Include Enough Detail**: As we cut and trim the descriptions of what we've done in the past, we can accidentally cut out too much information. You should view your resume as telling a story about how you've advanced in your career. The goal is to show a prospective employer that you have the ability to grow in any role. Make sure that your resume has enough details about what you've done in each position.

- **Don't Be Ambiguous**: The older a product manager gets, the more likely it is that we'll start to fudge some of the information contained in our resume. Leaving off dates such as when we graduated from college is a common technique in order to obscure our age. Don't do it, if the company decided to hire you they'll verify your degree(s) and so you should include graduation dates to begin with.

- **Grammar Counts:** Those squiggly red lines and green lines that show up as you are typing up your resume in Microsoft Word really do mean something. No matter how impressive your past accomplishments are, if your resume is littered with misspelled words or poorly constructed sentences then that will take away from how you are perceived.

What All Of This Means For You

In this age of Internet everything, product managers might think that all that it will take to get their next job is to have an account on every social networking site out there. It turns out that the old standby, your resume, is still an important communication tool.

Not only does it matter what work experiences you've had, but how you structure your resume and what information you put in it are what will make it work for you. Make sure that you include the essential details about your past jobs, eliminate any ambiguous information, and make sure that there are no spelling or grammatical errors.

Every job that you apply for ends up being a competition between you and other candidates. In order to give yourself the best possible advantage, you need to make sure that your resume does a good job of clearly telling your story. Follow these suggestions and you'll be well on your way...

Chapter 9

Product Managers With No Time Find A Quicker Way To Get An MBA

Chapter 9: Product Managers With No Time Find A Quicker Way To Get An MBA

As product managers who live in troubling times we are always trying to do two things: hold on to our jobs and make our product more successful. One of the best ways to do both of these, or so we have been told, is to go out and get an MBA. Well that's all great and fine if you've got four or five years to burn, don't need to do anything else at night, oh and have a big chunk of cash sitting around that you had no other plans for. Maybe it's time to look for a better way to accomplish what we're trying to do...

Say Hello To The Alternative To The MBA

Before you decide to quit your product manager job and go back to school in order to get an MBA (really, really expensive) or start going to night school to get an MBA (just really expensive), maybe you should take a moment and consider all of your options. Maybe what you really want is a specialized Master's degree.

Yeah, yeah – I know what you are thinking. We've all been drinking the "get an MBA" Kool-Aid for so long that it's hard to imagine doing anything else. However, depending on what you want to do with your life, this might actually be a better solution for you.

If having spent time being a product manager has gotten you interested in business, than getting an advanced business degree of some sort is probably a good idea. However, one of the things that keeps us from doing this is often the time involved to get the degree.

The Appeal Of Specializing

Business schools are starting to get the message. They are beginning to offer more and more specialized business programs that are only 12 months long. In the 2008-2009 school year there were 645 programs offered. This is up from the 614 programs that had been offered just two years earlier.

What these types of degrees offer are parts of the typical MBA curriculum, but they are often more technical in nature and generally spend less time on general management skills.

Here in lies the rub: these types of specialty business degrees are not designed to get you promoted to eventually become the CEO. Rather what they are designed to do is to sharpen your business skills in a narrow area and make you more valuable to the company in your current job.

This type of continuing education especially appeals to new product managers: those who don't have the five years of work experience that most MBA programs require for entrance. No matter if this is your case, or if you've just found some part of the product management job that you are really drawn to, a narrowly focused master's degree might be just the ticket for you.

What To Do With Your New Degree

Ok, so let's say that you bite the bullet and run off and skip the MBA and instead get a very focused master's degree in marketing, finance, or some other business discipline. What then?

It turns out that taking this path, might feel like the right thing for you to do, but as they like to say on TV, your results may vary. Since specialty master's degrees are not as well-known as

MBA's you're going to have to deal with some lack of recognition issues.

Although it may change in the future, right now MBA students still seem to get the best deal when it comes to getting the economic benefits from going through the effort of getting an advanced degree. The people who design the GMAT test that everyone takes to get admitted to graduate programs are reporting that MBA students are saying that they get a 73% increase in salary after graduating while students with specialty master's degrees are only reporting a 26% increase.

What All Of This Means For You

In the end the decision rests with you. We all know that continuing our education is an important thing for every product manager to do. Going back to school almost seems like a no-brainer until you realize that you need to spend some time thinking about just what you want to get out of doing so.

A specialty master's degree offers product managers who have been working for less than five years or who found one particular part of the job most interesting with a new option. By investing 12 months of study, they can walk away with both another degree as well as a deep understanding of one area of business.

The value of taking this educational route will really depend on the career that you want for yourself. If you are comfortable working inside of the business instead of running it, then a specialty master's degree might be the right way to go for you!

Chapter 10

How To Really Screw Up Your Next Product Manager Job Search

Chapter 10: How To Really Screw Up Your Next Product Manager Job Search

Product managers may be very good at managing a product and making it a success in the marketplace; however, all too often we do a really bad job of looking for our next job. I'm not talking about poorly formatted resumes or even answering questions incorrectly during a job interview. My point is that it's all the other actions that we take during a job search that really end up shooting ourselves in the foot. Still confused? Maybe I should explain myself...

The Problem With Black Lists

When you are in the middle of a job search, it's pretty easy to start to think about the firms that you are trying to get an interview with as being these big, impersonal "things". In reality, you are really dealing with a small group of people that can include recruiters and members of the company's HR staff.

Working as a product manager has conditioned all of us to view the world in pretty narrow terms: things either work or they don't. We have a bad habit of bringing this view to our job search. This is what can get us into hot water.

It turns out that all of the people involved in the hiring process, recruiters, HR staff, etc. all talk to each other. When we tick them off, they'll put our name on their personal "black list" and then life just got a lot harder. This is something that we tend to forget.

Reasons That We Screw Up

When we think that we're being clever and trying to get a job interview with a company by going in through the front door (job postings on their web site) and the back door (with a recruiter) at the same time, we end up making everyone mad at us.

Recruiters don't like it when you've gone direct because they don't make any money if they place you and the company already knew about you. HR staff don't like having your name show up multiple times for the same position. What can happen very quickly is that your name gets placed on a "black list" .

Once your name is on the unofficial black list, you'll find that recruiters won't return your calls (they talk to each other also) and the company won't acknowledge your emails.

How To Fix Problems That You've Made

Getting off of a black list once you've landed there is very difficult. First off, you need to understand that it's going to take time to get off of the list. It took time to get on the list, it's only fair that it should take time to get off of it.

Your first action should be to stop doing whatever got you black listed in the first place. Just because you soured your relationship with one recruiter doesn't mean that you have to compound the problem with other recruiters.

Next, you need to find ways to be a giver, not a taker with the recruiter / HR staff that you've offended. This doesn't mean sending them gifts – those look fake anyway. Instead, you should look for ways to make their jobs easier. One way would be to send them highly qualified candidates for their open positions (no – you can't recommend yourself). Also, acting as a good reference for someone that they are considering can also win you points.

Things You Should Never Do

We are living in the 21st Century and that means that the number of ways that you can hurt your job search effort have multiplied. Here's a quick list of other things that you should never do:

- Don't post anything on Facebook, Instagram or any other social media site that you wouldn't want your mother to read / see.

- Don't bend the truth in your resume.

- Don't spam the world with your resume.

- Don't submit the same cover letter for multiple positions in the same company.

- Don't send your resume to multiple recruiters and HR hiring managers at the same company.

- Don't apply for jobs for which you don't even meet the basic requirements.

- Don't send your resume to the same recruiters over, and over, and over again.

What All Of This Means For You

Looking for your next job has always been a challenge. In today's online hyper-connected world, some things have become easier while others have become much more difficult.

It's all too easy to become too eager when looking for your next product management job. If you work with too many people or send your resume out too far and wide then you risk being black listed by recruiters and hiring managers.

Keep your job search focused and stay honest with what you tell people about yourself. You will find that next job but only if you treat the people who will help you to find it with respect.

Chapter 11

To Get Your Next Job, You Need To Know How Firms Hire Product Managers

Chapter 11: To Get Your Next Job, You Need To Know How Firms Hire Product Managers

So what's your job status? You either currently have a job (yea!) or you are looking for your next one (yea!) There is no shortage of job search advice out there on the Internet and otherwise. They've pretty much said all that there is to say about resumes, dressing nicely, researching the company, etc. How about if we talk about something different – how the company that you've applied to actually goes about filling their open positions?

Making The First Cut

Going for a job at a company is very much like trying to win a gold medal at the Olympics: many will try, but only one will win. Just imagine what the company that has the job opening is going to have to go through in order to sort out all of the applicants that they get for every open spot.

The first thing that you need to realize is that the first pass of work to weed out the clearly unqualified candidates will be done most likely by a team. This will be a bunch of employees / contractors who may not know much about the specific job, but who have been told what to look for in resumes and cover letters.

Product managers who want to get past this first cut need to include a cover letter. Your cover letter needs to contain two important pieces of information: you need to include words that talk about how you meet the key qualifications that were identified in the job posting and you need to include key words that have to do with this job.

Next Step: The Phone Interview

Whenever we apply for a job, time instantly becomes our enemy. If you become worried that your application for the job never got to the firm, then it is socially permissible to make a follow-up call to ask for confirmation after 5 days have passed.

You've probably heard this before, but the best way to get your next job is to connect with actual people instead of just submitting your resume to a firm. Candidates who come in via a recommendation from an employee or a trusted source often get to bypass the first round of applicant cuts.

Firms generally end up with a list of about 20 candidates or so that they'll take to the next round: the phone interview. From the company's perspective the phone interview has two missions: to make sure that you understand what the job is and to make sure that it lines up with your salary expectations.

However, there is another reason for a phone interview. It give the company a chance to evaluate your communication skills – are you a good talker, do you seem confidant?

Last Step: The Face-To-Face Interview & Selection

Every firm differs, but a good rule of thumb is that about 6 candidates are granted interviews for a given opening. Once all of the prospective candidates have completed their interviews, it's time for the company to make a decision.

The actual hiring manager will meet with all of the people who participated in the interviews in order to get their recommendation for who should be hired. The key here is that they get only opinions, the final decision still rests in the hands of the hiring manager. This final selection is more often than not based on two criteria: how well your skills and experience fit the job and how much enthusiasm you showed during the interview process.

What All Of This Means For You

Interviewing for a new job is a numbers game: it's you against the rest of the world. Knowing what goes on inside of the company that is doing the hiring can be your key to getting the job that you want.

A good cover letter will get you past the first round of cuts. However, you're going to have to do well on the phone interview in order to get invited in for a face-to-face interview.

In the end, how much you've studied the firm and the job will determine your chances. Make sure that you let the interviewers know how excited you are about the challenges that come along with the job and you'll be that much closer to being hired...

Chapter 12

Oh, Oh – What To Do When You Don't Get That Promotion

Chapter 12: Oh, Oh – What To Do When You Don't Get That Promotion

Things are tough all over. If you were counting on getting a promotion this year, you might want to scale your hopes back just a bit. A lot of product managers are discovering that their career plans are having to be put on hold. Maybe we should spend some time talking about what you should do now...

The Root Of The Problem

Have you noticed just how far down the U.S. stock market has dropped over the last couple of years? Since most of the baby boomer generation that is currently working has their retirement funds tied up in stocks, they've seen their dreams of a well-funded retirement take a hit. What this means is that they won't be retiring any time soon.

What this means for product managers is that the normal process of staff retiring each year and opening up senior management positions that are then filled by junior staff won't be happening this year. Dang!

The folks over at Watson Wyatt Worldwide Inc. have done a survey of more than 2,200 U.S. employees and they've found that 44% of workers who are over 50 plan on postponing their retirement. Just to make things even worse, about half of these folks are now planning on working at least three years longer than they had originally planned on.

The Promotion Problem

So let's talk frankly here: no matter what level your product management career is currently at, you are going to be blocked.

Just to make things even worse, the experts are telling us that we shouldn't expect promotions to come back any time soon.

So what should you do? Quit? In this economy? I don't think so. Instead we should take a look and see if we can come up with a different solution.

As always, if you are expecting a promotion and you don't get it, you need to take a look at the underlying reasons for you not getting the promotion. If you determine that your promotion was postponed because of either the company's economic situation is poor or because there is a human logjam before you, then you still have hope.

Now you've got to plot your next step.

Solutions

The easiest way to solve this problem is if you are willing to accept an alternative to a promotion – like money. This is sometimes called a "retention reward" and it's a bonus that is paid to employees when they deserve a promotion but one is not currently possible.

Once you realize that your deserved promotion may be delayed, you need to start to take steps to boost your value to the company. What you really want to do is to make it very easy for the company to slide you into the promotion once it becomes available. This means having a talk with your boss in order to find out if there are ways to get some of the experience that goes along with the promotion position even if you can't get the title right now.

As with all requests like this, you do need to be careful. You don't want the company to get too comfortable with you doing the work of the higher level position while being paid at your current lower rate.

What All Of This Means For You

The world is working against you – just when you are expecting a promotion, everything gets flipped upside down and you find your way up the career ladder blocked. These things happen and you need to find ways to deal with it.

Quitting is always an option; however, unless you have another job already lined up it's probably not the way to go right now. Instead, ask if you can get a bonus to replace the promotion that you won't be getting right now. At the same time see if there is any way that you can gain more experience doing the type of work that you will be doing when the promotions free up once again.

Promotions will eventually return. As a top-notch product manager you need to use this delay to build the skills that will ensure that you will be one of the first to get promoted once things start moving again. Take these actions now and you'll be ready for the big day whenever it finally comes...

It's from the forge of failure that the steel of success is formed.

Hard Work Does Not Guarantee Success, But Success Does Not Happen Without Hard Work.

- Dr. Jim Anderson

Create Products Your Customers Want At A Price That They Are Willing To Pay!

Dr. Jim Anderson is available to provide training and coaching on the two topics that are the most important to product managers everywhere: how do I create the products that my customers want and what should I price them at?

Dr. Anderson believes that in order to both learn and remember what he says, product managers need to laugh. Each one of his speeches is full of fun and humor so that what he says "sticks" with everyone.

Dr. Anderson's Product Management Training Includes:

1. How can you segment your market?
2. What problems are your customers having right now?
3. Which of your customer's problems does your product solve?
4. How much of this problem does your product solve?
5. How much will it cost your customer if they don't fix this problem?

Dr. Jim Anderson presents over 100 speeches per year. To invite Dr. Anderson to speak at your event, contact him at:

Phone: 813-418-6970 or
Email: jim@BlueElephantConsulting.com

Blue
Elephant
Consulting

Speaking.   Negotiating.   Managing.   Marketing.

Photo Credits:

Cover - By: University of Salford Press Office
http://www.flickr.com/photos/salforduniversity/
Chapter 1 - By: Michael Heiss
https://www.flickr.com/photos/michaelheiss/

Chapter 2 – By: James Lee
https://www.flickr.com/photos/jronaldlee/

Chapter 3 – By : Paul Inkles
https://www.flickr.com/photos/dumfstar/

Chapter 4 – By : le temple du chemisier
https://www.flickr.com/photos/9110880@N04/

Chapter 5 – By : Ann Powell Groner
https://www.flickr.com/photos/apgroner/

Chapter 6 – By : Todd Dwyer
https://www.flickr.com/photos/ret0dd/

Chapter 7 – By : Brian Ujiie
https://www.flickr.com/photos/bujiie/

Chapter 8 – By : Flazingo Photos
https://www.flickr.com/photos/124247024@N07/

Chapter 9 – By : Madeline Wright
https://www.flickr.com/photos/madaroni/

Chapter 10 – By : Allain Gavillet
https://www.flickr.com/photos/trams-lisbonne/

Chapter 11 – By : Flazingo Photos
https://www.flickr.com/photos/124247024@N07/

Chapter 12 – By : Johan Hansson
https://www.flickr.com/photos/plastanka/with/15003109277/

Other Books By The Author

Product Management

- Product Management Secrets: Techniques For Product Managers To Boost Product Sales And Increase Customer Satisfaction

- Product Development Lessons For Product Managers: How Product Managers Can Create Successful Products

- Customer Lessons For Product Managers: Techniques For Product Managers To Better Understand What Their Customers Really Want

- Product Failure Lessons For Product Managers: Examples Of Products That Have Failed For Product Managers To Learn From

- Communication Skills For Product Managers: The Communication Skills That Product Managers Need To Know How To Use In Order To Have A Successful Product

- How To Have A Successful Product Manager Career: The Things That You Need To Be Doing TODAY In Order To Have A Successful Product Manager Career

- Product Manager Product Success: How to keep your product on track and make it become a success

Public Speaking

- How To Become A Better Speaker By Changing How You Speak: Change techniques that will transform a speech into a memorable event

- How To Give A Great Presentation: Presentation techniques that will transform a speech into a memorable event

- How To Rehearse In Order To Give The Perfect Speech: How to effectively rehearse your next speech to that your message be remembered forever!

- Secrets To Creating The Perfect Speech: How to create a speech that will make your message be remembered forever!

- Secrets To Organizing The Perfect Speech: How to organize the best speech of your life!

- Secrets To Planning The Perfect Speech: How to plan to give the best speech of your life

- How To Show What You Mean During A Presentation: How to use visual techniques to transform a speech into a memorable event

CIO Skills

- What CIOs Need To Know About Working With Partners: Techniques For CIOs To Use In Order To Be Able To Successfully Work With Partners

- Critical CIO Management Skills: Decision Making Skills That Every CIO Needs To Have In Order To Be Able To Make The Right Choices

- How CIOs Can Make Innovation Happen: Tips And Techniques For CIOs To Use In Order To Make Innovation Happen In Their IT Department

- CIO Communication Skills Secrets: Tips And Techniques For CIOs To Use In Order To Become Better Communicators

- Managing Your CIO Career: Steps That CIOs Have To Take In Order To Have A Long And Successful Career

- CIO Business Skills: How CIOs can work effectively with the rest of the company!

IT Manager Skills

- How IT Managers Can Make Innovation Happen: Tips And Techniques For IT Managers To Use In Order To Make Innovation Happen In Their Teams

- Staffing Skills IT Managers Must Have: Tips And Techniques That IT Managers Can Use In Order To Correctly Staff Their Teams

- Secrets Of Effective Leadership For IT Managers: Tips And Techniques That IT Managers Can Use In Order To Develop Leadership Skills

- IT Manager Career Secrets: Tips And Techniques That IT Managers Can Use In Order To Have A Successful Career

- IT Manager Budgeting Skills: How IT Managers Can Request, Manage, Use, And Track Their Funding

Negotiating

- Learn How To Signal In Your Next Negotiation: How To Develop The Skill Of Effective Signaling In A Negotiation In Order To Get The Best Possible Outcome

- Learn The Skill Of Exploring In A Negotiation: How To Develop The Skill Of Exploring What Is Possible In A Negotiation In Order To Reach The Best Possible Deal

- Learn How To Argue In Your Next Negotiation: How To Develop The Skill Of Effective Arguing In A Negotiation In Order To Get The Best Possible Outcome

- How To Open Your Next Negotiation: How To Start A Negotiation In Order To Get The Best Possible Outcome

- Preparing For Your Next Negotiation: What You Need To Do BEFORE A Negotiation Starts In Order To Get The Best Possible Deal

Miscellaneous

- The Internet-Enabled Successful School District Superintendent: How To Use The Internet To Boost Parental Involvement In Your Schools

- Power Distribution Unit (PDU) Secrets: What Everyone Who Works In A Data Center Needs To Know!

- Making The Jump: How To Land Your Dream Job When You Get Out Of College!

"Practical, proven examples of how to secure the right product management job and be a success!"

This book has been written with one goal in mind – to show you how to find the right product management job for you. We're going to show you how to make sure that this job turns into a success for you!

Let's Make Your Career A Success!

What You'll Find Inside:

- **YOUR MOTHER WAS RIGHT: HOW PRODUCT MANAGERS DRESS FOR SUCCES**

- **GROW YOUR CAREER – WHAT PRODUCT MANAGERS NEED TO DO FOR SUCCESS**

- **HOW TO BUILD A MENTOR NETWORK FOR YOUR PRODUCT MANAGEMENT CAREER**

- **TO GET YOUR NEXT JOB, YOU NEED TO KNOW HOW FIRMS HIRE PRODUCT MANAGERS**

Dr. Jim Anderson brings his 4 college degrees coupled with over 25 years of real-world experience to this book. He's managed products at some of the world's largest firms as well as at start-ups. He's going to show you what you need to do in order to make your career a success!

www.ingramcontent.com/pod-product-compliance
Lightning Source LLC
Chambersburg PA
CBHW071304170526
45165CB00003B/1412